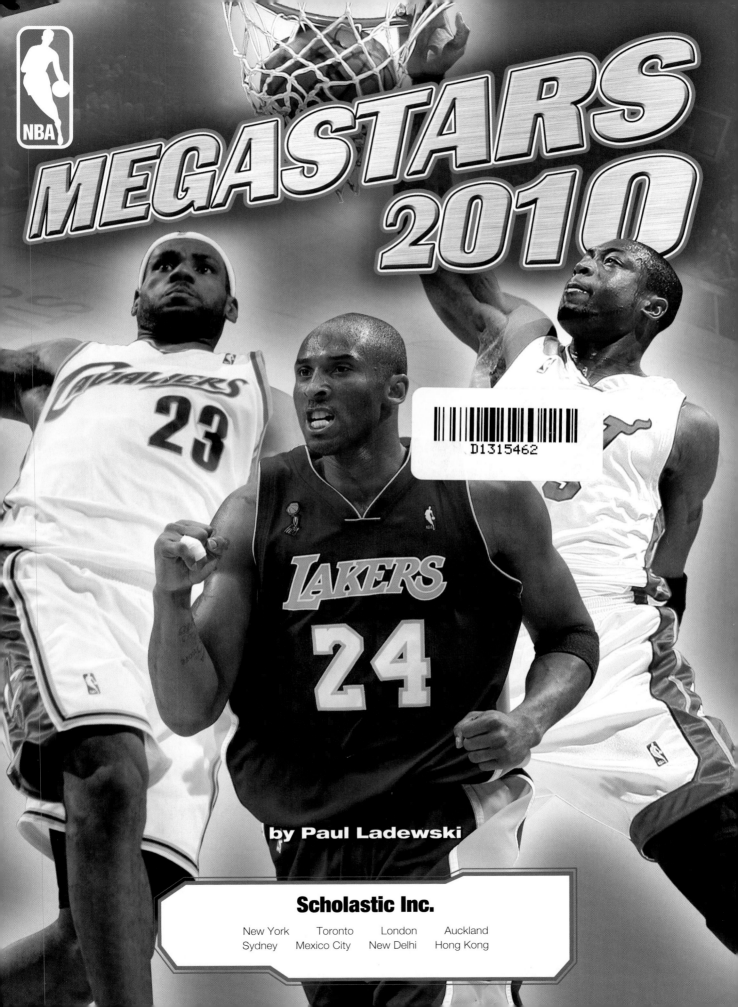

NBA MEGASTARS 2010

by Paul Ladewski

Scholastic Inc.

New York   Toronto   London   Auckland
Sydney   Mexico City   New Delhi   Hong Kong

Photos:

Front cover (left to right): LeBron James © NBAE/Getty Images;
Kobe Bryant © Sports Illustrated/Getty Images;
Dwyane Wade © NBAE/Getty Images

Back cover (left to right): Carmelo Anthony © Getty Images,
Dirk Nowitzki © NBAE/Getty Images, Kevin Garnett © NBAE/Getty Images

Interior: (3, 11-12, 18, 26, 31) © Getty Images; (5-10, 13-17, 19-20, 22-25, 27, 29)
© NBAE/Getty Images; (21) © AFP/Getty Images; (28) © Bongarts/Getty Images;
(30) © Sports Illustrated/Getty Images; (4, 32) © WireImage/Getty Images

No part of this work may be reproduced, stored in a retrieval system, or transmitted in any form or by
any means, electronic, mechanical, photocopying, recording, or otherwise without written permission
of the publisher. For information regarding permission, write to Scholastic Inc., Attention: Permissions
Department, 557 Broadway, New York, NY 10012.

ISBN 978-0-545-20648-8

The NBA and individual NBA member team identifications, photographs, and other content used on or
in this publication are trademarks, copyrighted designs, and other forms of intellectual property of NBA
Properties, Inc., and the respective NBA member teams and may not be used, in whole or part, without
the prior written consent of NBA Properties, Inc. All rights reserved.

Copyright © 2010 by NBA Properties, Inc.

All rights reserved. Published by Scholastic Inc. SCHOLASTIC and associated logos are trademarks and/
or registered trademarks of Scholastic Inc.

12 11 10 9 8 7 6 5 4 3 2 1   10 11 12 13 14 15/0

Designed by Cheung Tai
Printed in the U.S.A.   40
First printing, January 2010

KOBE BRYANT

KOBE BRYANT

In 12 seasons of professional basketball, Los Angeles Lakers superstar guard Kobe Bryant has been just about everywhere, done just about everything.

All-Star Game? Been there 11 times. Top scorer in the league? Did that four times. NBA Playoffs? Been there 12 times.

But last season Kobe did something that he had never done before.

He carried the Lakers to the NBA title as their team leader. He averaged 32.4 points per game in the championship series and was elected NBA Finals Most Valuable Player for the first time in his career.

Now Kobe is known as more than just a great player. He's a great winner, too.

"There's plenty left," Kobe promised Lakers fans while they chanted "M-V-P! M-V-P!" at the victory celebration last June. "We're a young team, a team that has a lot of chemistry. And we're all hungry. We want to do this again and again . . ."

Even before Kobe Bean Bryant became one of the best basketball players ever, he had been to many places in the world. He was born on August 23, 1978, in Philadelphia, Pennsylvania where his father, Joe, was an NBA player for four seasons. When Kobe was six years old, his family moved to Europe, where he learned to speak Italian and play soccer and basketball.

Several years later, the Bryants returned to the Philadelphia area, where Kobe led the Lower Merion High School team to the state championship. Rather than attend Duke on a scholarship, the 17-year-old became the first guard to jump from high school to professional basketball.

"We're gonna keep on rollin'."

In 1996, the Charlotte Hornets drafted Kobe with the 13th pick in the first round. Before he played his first NBA game, the Lakers acquired him in a trade. It turned out to be one of the best deals that they ever made.

Years later, Kobe has found a home in Southern California, where he has been a part of four NBA championship teams. Now that the Lakers team captain has a ring for each finger on one hand, he wants one for his thumb.

"We'll be ready to go," Kobe promises. "We're gonna keep on rollin'."

LEBRON JAMES

LEBRON JAMES

When Michael Jordan played his final game, many experts predicted that basketball would not see anyone like him for many years, maybe ever.

LeBron James was only 18 years old at the time, so how could they know that the next Air Jordan might be just getting started?

It's too early to say that LeBron will catch Michael eventually. After all, Michael averaged more points per game (30.1) than any player in NBA history. His teams also won six league championships. Even so, in six seasons, LeBron is off to a flying start.

LeBron Raymone James was born on December 30, 1984, in Akron, Ohio. "I was blessed with a God-given talent, and my mother raised me the right way," he says. LeBron attended St. Vincent-St. Mary High School and was selected Mr. Basketball in the state three times.

After LeBron chose to turn pro rather than attend college, the Cavaliers selected him as the first overall pick in the 2003 NBA Draft. Since then, he has been named NBA Rookie of the Year and NBA All-Star Game Most Valuable Player two times.

LeBron has long been known as one of the greatest athletes in the world, but last season he started to be recognized as a winner as well. In the 2008-09 season, LeBron carried the Cavaliers to 66 victories, by far the most in their history.

"Sometimes the coaches tell me to be selfish, but my game won't let me be selfish," LeBron explains.

As the Most Valuable Player in the league, LeBron was simply the best. Most players would like to have even one game of 28 points, eight rebounds, seven assists, two steals, and one blocked shot in their careers. For LeBron, that was an average game in the regular season! LeBron still has a lot on his to-do list to catch Michael, but he has plenty of time to get it done.

> **"Sometimes the coaches tell me to be selfish, but my game won't let me be selfish."**

DWYANE WADE

Most star athletes were noticed for their talent at a young age, but Dwyane Wade wasn't one of them. It wasn't until his junior year in high school that he started to come into his own as a basketball player. He chose to attend Marquette University, one of only three colleges that were interested in him.

Dwyane already owns an NBA championship ring, has played in five All-Star Games, and has been the top scorer in the league once. Because Dwyane Tyrone Wade has accomplished so much in such a short amount of time, one would think that he doesn't practice as much anymore, right? No way. Even in the summer, Dwyane can often be found in his "office", where he works to improve his game.

"I like to be in the gym working on different stuff by myself — just me and nobody else," Dwyane says. "That's when I get a lot done."

Dwyane's drive to improve his game definitely paid off. In the summer of '08, he practiced his three-pointer shot from beyond the arc for hours at a time. *Presto!* Not only did Dwyane sink more three-balls than ever before last season, he also scored more points than any player in the league.

Born in Chicago, Illinois on January 17, 1982, Dwyane is called Flash because of his lightning-quick moves that allow him to blow past a defender. When Flash gets close to the basket, he can twist and turn his body in a way that allows him to get off a shot — and usually make it.

As Dwyane explains, "I'm the type of player who goes off the dribble, and that's when I make up moves or try to imitate moves I've seen."

> **"I'm the type of player who goes off the dribble, and that's when I make up moves or try to imitate moves I've seen."**

Last season Dwyane played more minutes, scored more points, dished out more assists, and blocked more shots than at any other time in his career. Don't expect him to stop there, though. As Dwyane proves, if you want to be successful, dedication and determination are excellent qualities to have.

KEVIN GARNETT

KEVIN GARNETT

Think of the NBA championship as a puzzle. Now think of a team that has all the pieces except the most important one of all.

Now you know what it was like to be the Boston Celtics without Kevin Garnett late last season.

When the Celtics announced that Kevin would sit out of the playoffs because of a sore right knee, it was almost like someone had let the air out of a thousand party balloons. *Pfffffffff!* The Celtics couldn't replace his points, rebounds, and blocked shots. Plus, they missed his energy.

"It's not hard to give everything that I have," says Kevin, the 6-11 forward known as K.G. and The Big Ticket. "At the end of the day, it's about effort and heart."

Kevin Maurice Garnett was born on May 19, 1976, in Greenville, South Carolina. He grew up in Chicago, Illinois, where he attended Farragut Academy. A number of talented high school players have played in the Windy City over the years, but many consider Kevin to be the best of them all.

> **"At the end of the day, it's about effort and heart."**

In fact, Kevin was so skilled at such a young age that he did something that hadn't been done in 20 years. After graduation, he jumped directly from high school to the pros. In the 1995 Draft, the Minnesota Timberwolves selected him with the fifth overall pick.

Since then, Kevin has lived up to his potential. In the 2000 Olympics, he led the United States team to a gold medal. Four years later, he was selected Most Valuable Player in the league. He has averaged 20.2 points and 11.1 rebounds per game in his career.

Before the 2007-08 season, Kevin was traded to the Celtics in return for five players and two draft picks in one of the biggest deals in basketball history. Along with guard Ray Allen and forward Paul Pierce, K.G. led the Celtics to their 17th league championship — more than any team in the league.

Once Kevin recovers from his knee injury, the Celtics will once again have their missing puzzle piece and definitely have another run at an NBA championship.

CHRIS PAUL

As everyone knows, it doesn't pay to steal. Unless you're Chris Paul, that is. The New Orleans Hornets point guard has the quickest hands in the league.

Last season Chris swiped the ball from the other team 216 times — more than anyone in the league. In fact, few players have ever done it better. When Chris played his 107th consecutive game with a steal last season, he set an NBA record.

> **"I really pride myself on when I get a deflection not to let the other team come up with it."**

Chris is quicker than a hiccup. When the ball is loose on the floor, he is usually the first player to get his busy hands on it. "I like to steal the ball," Chris says. "I really pride myself on when I get a deflection not to let the other team come up with it."

Christopher Emmanuel Paul was born on May 6, 1985, in Winston-Salem, North Carolina. At West Forsyth High School, he was named Mr. Basketball in the state. In his two years at Wake Forest University, his team played in the NCAA Tournament both times.

In the 2005 NBA Draft, the Hornets selected Chris with the fourth pick. In his first season, he was selected as NBA Rookie of the Year. Now many consider him to be the best point guard in the league.

Known as CP3, his initials and uniform number, Chris works hard to be the best. By paying close attention to the moves of his opponents, he knows what to expect before it happens.

"That's one thing I've always done since high school, just knowing the game, knowing what plays that teams are running and understanding where guys are trying to pass the ball," says Chris, who likes to bowl, listen to music, and bike in the mountains in his spare time.

As the Hornets floor leader, Chris does many things for his team. Last season he finished fifth in the Most Valuable Player vote, higher than any player in his position. An excellent passer who can dribble to the rim with ease, he also led the league in assists. He is a dead-eye on outside shots.

In Chris Paul, the Hornets got a steal themselves, one might say.

TONY PARKER

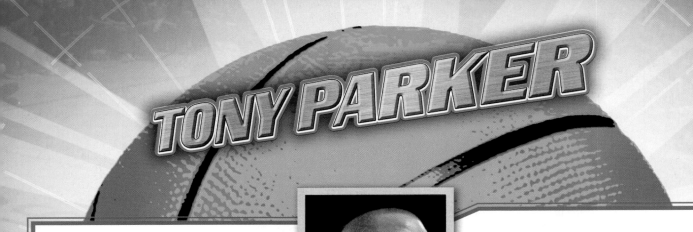

San Antonio Spurs star Tony Parker has come a long, long way in eight seasons. First, he traveled more than 5,000 miles from France to begin his NBA career. Then Tony went from a raw rookie who lacked confidence to one of the best point guards in the league to a slick ballhandler that can score on layups and floaters, or dish the ball to a teammate for an open shot.

In the 2008-09 season, Tony was better than ever. While teammates Manu Ginobili and Tim Duncan were in and out of the Spurs line-up because of injuries, he stepped up to average 22.0 points and 6.9 assists per game, the best numbers of his career.

"I am satisfied with what I did, but as usual, I do not wish to stop here," Tony says. "I still want to go higher, and my goal is to improve each year in order to become the best possible basketball player. I do not give myself any limit."

William Anthony Parker was born on May 17, 1982, in Bruges, Belgium. His father, Tony, was a very good basketball player in Europe, where he taught Little Tony and his two younger brothers how to play the game.

Because Tony decided to stay overseas rather than attend a major college, his name was not well-known in the United States before the 2001 Draft. The Spurs had the 28th pick in the first round, and when he was available there, they were quick to take him.

Years later, Tony remains very popular in France, where he plays for the

"I do not give myself any limit."

national team in international competitions. When Tony is in a public place, photographers usually aren't far behind him.

"I'm used to it a little bit," Tony shrugs. "When I go back to France, it's crazy. Everywhere I go, it's like a lot of people and paparazzi. So I just stay with my bodyguard and go into private restaurants and stuff like that."

Tony feels most comfortable on a basketball court, where he doesn't need anyone to protect him. He has such super-quick moves, few if any opponents can touch him there.

YAO MING

YAO MING

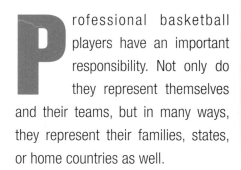

Professional basketball players have an important responsibility. Not only do they represent themselves and their teams, but in many ways, they represent their families, states, or home countries as well.

Yao Ming carries the hopes of more than 1.3 billion people.

Yao Ming was born on September 12, 1980, in Shanghai, China, a country with such a large population that about one out of every five people in the world lives there. Expectations were quite large for Yao as he entered the NBA for the 2002-03 season.

"All of the Chinese people, the Asian people say, 'Oh, Yao Ming, you are all the Chinese, all of Asia's hopes,'" Yao says. "That's a lot of pressure. I'm just a basketball player."

In 2002, Yao was the first international player without any U.S. experience to be selected with the No. 1 overall pick of the NBA Draft. As one might expect, it was not easy for him to play basketball in a new land at first. "Moving to the U.S. was quite a

> **"That's a lot of pressure. I'm just a basketball player."**

transition for me to say the least!" Yao once said. "There were and still are so many new things to get used to — the language, food, culture, even the style of basketball is different here!"

Yao caught on very quickly, though. In seven seasons with the Houston Rockets, he was selected to play in the All-Star Game each time. The All-Star center can score anywhere within 18 feet of the basket. Plus, he has learned to become a skilled passer.

Yao's most recent season saw him average 19.9 points, 9.9 rebounds, and 1.9 blocked shots per game. He sank more than half his field-goal attempts and about seven of every eight free-throw tries.

The Rockets won 53 games in the regular season, and then advanced to the second round of the playoffs. If Yao hadn't gone down because of a fractured left foot, they might have gone farther. Yao is recovering from that fractured foot and can't wait to get back on the basketball court.

To millions of people overseas, it can't happen soon enough.

BRANDON ROY

BRANDON ROY

Just as nobody reaches the top of Mount Everest in a matter of hours, no team climbs from last place to the NBA championship in one season. It takes a lot of talent and hard work, plus it doesn't hurt to have Brandon Roy on your team.

Even though Brandon Roy and the Portland Trail Blazers didn't advance past the first round of the

"All of our guys are happy we had a great season. . ."

playoffs last season, the young bunch took some impressive steps toward their goal.

"A great experience for us," Brandon called the series against the more experienced Houston Rockets, who beat the Trail Blazers in six hard-fought games. "All of our guys are happy we had a great season, but they have a bad taste in their mouth, because we feel like we could have played better this series."

You can tell a lot about a player by the way he performs in big games. In his first trip to the playoffs, Brandon came through like a

veteran. The guard commonly referred to as B Roy averaged 26.7 points per game, nearly four more than he did in the regular season.

Born on July 23, 1984, in Seattle, Washington, Brandon Dawayne Roy is wise beyond his years. While attending the University of Washington in Seattle for four years, Brandon was able to spend more time in the classroom and improve his game at the same time.

In the 2005-06 season, the Trail Blazers had the worst record in the league. In need of a young player to build around in the future, they acquired Brandon in a trade with the Minnesota Timberwolves on the night of the 2006 NBA Draft.

In Brandon, the Trail Blazers got exactly what they needed — a natural leader who doesn't wow people with fancy moves but plays at a high level almost every game. At 6-6, he can shoot over smaller opponents, drive around bigger ones, or dish the ball to an open teammate when two defenders come after him.

Slowly but surely, Brandon and the Trail Blazers have moved forward together, from 21 victories to 32 to 41 to 54 last season. They're not at the top of the mountain quite yet, but it's definitely in their reach.

KEVIN DURANT

Even as a kid, Kevin Durant knew his way around the court. So maybe it's no surprise that the bright, young star of the Oklahoma City Thunder finds his way around a basketball court so easily.

Born on September 29, 1988, in Washington, D.C., Kevin Wayne Durant took up basketball at a young age. "My mom thought it would be a fun activity to keep me away from the streets," he says. In four years, he starred at three different high schools.

"My mom thought it would be a fun activity to keep me away from the streets."

In college, Kevin carried the University of Texas to the second round of the NCAA Tournament. As the first freshman to be selected College Player of the Year, he was ready to move on to the next level already. In the 2007 NBA Draft, the Seattle SuperSonics chose him at the second pick. After Kevin was selected Rookie of the Year, he moved to Oklahoma City along with the rest of the team.

Kevin is listed as a forward-guard, which is fitting because he can pretty much play anywhere on the court. Then again, how many stand 6-9, weigh 215 pounds, and have arms that extend nearly 7 1/2 feet? Kevin has the size and length to play close to the basket, where he's the Thunder down under. He's slender and quick enough to play away from the hoop as well.

Many experts consider Kevin to be Tracy McGrady and Dirk Nowitzki rolled into one player.

Like Tracy, the Houston Rockets guard, Kevin is a good ball-handler and excellent outside shooter. Last season he worked hard to improve his jump shot from beyond the three-point arc. After hours of practice, he became one of the best long-range threats in the league and averaged 25.3 points per game.

Like Dirk, the Dallas Mavericks forward, Kevin is a good rebounder. Better not leave either one alone around the free-throw circle, or else he'll play string music all night long. Kevin has had such a great start — one can only imagine where his game will take him in the future.

DWIGHT HOWARD

DWIGHT HOWARD

Once upon a time, professional basketball was dominated by the tallest players closest to the basket. As the rules and athletes began to change, the game drifted away from the hoop. Now there is more emphasis on speed, quickness, and shot-makers in the wide, open spaces. Just don't tell that to Dwight Howard.

At 6-11 and 265 pounds, Dwight is the most dominant inside force in the game. When Howard gets the ball in the paint, it practically takes a tractor to budge him. Last season he dunked the ball 202 times — more than any player in the league.

In the 2008 Slam Dunk Contest, Dwight made a shot that is still talked about today. First, he put on a Superman cape, then he soared through the air from a few inches inside the free-throw line and threw the ball through the hoop. Fans voted and he was declared the winner of the contest.

"Blocking shots, changing shots, and being effective on the defensive end is more dominating than having 30 points."

Dwight does more than dunk the ball. At the other end of the court, Superman is super, *man*. He was selected Defensive Player of the Year last season, when he averaged 13.8 rebounds and 2.9 blocked shots per game — the most in the league.

"Blocking shots, changing shots, and being effective on the defensive end is more dominating than having 30 points," Dwight says. "It's not always about scoring, especially with me."

Dwight D. Howard II attended Southwest Christian Academy in Atlanta, Georgia where he was born on December 8, 1985. In his senior year, he led his team to the state championship.

Like Kevin Garnett, one of his favorite players, Dwight made the jump from high school to the pros. In the 2004 NBA Draft, the Magic selected him at the first pick. He has appeared in three All-Star Games since then.

JOE JOHNSON

The Atlanta Hawks are a young, athletic team, and one of the most fun to watch in professional basketball. It takes more than that to win the big prize, though. It also takes experience and leadership, the kind that Joe Johnson has given his team the last four seasons.

The rise of the Hawks can be traced to August 19, 2005, the day that Joe was acquired from the Phoenix Suns in a trade. "I think this is going to be fun for all of us players," he predicted. "We'll have so many athletic guys who can get up and down the floor. And it will be great for the fans. We're going to be an exciting team."

Joe is a steady player, not a flashy one, and he would rather have his jump shot speak for him. In his first season in a Hawks uniform, the 6-7 guard led the team in minutes, points, assists, and steals. He also set an example with his drive, determination, and positive attitude. The team won 26 games, exactly twice as many as the season before.

Slowly but surely, rung by rung, the Hawks climbed the ladder of success. Marvin Williams and Al Horford joined whiz kid Josh Smith in the draft, and Joe helped teach them how to become professionals. Last season the team advanced to the second round of the playoffs for the first time in 10 years.

Born on June 29, 1981, Joe Marcus Johnson has Arkansas roots. He attended Little Rock Central High School and the University of Arkansas. In the 2001 NBA Draft, the Boston Celtics selected him in the first round. Two years later, he was traded to the Suns and soon became one of the best three-point shooters in the league.

> **"We'll have so many athletic guys who can get up and down the floor. And it will be great for the fans. We're going to be an exciting team."**

Still, Joe believed that he was capable of more. When he had a chance to move to Atlanta, a place where he could grow with his teammates close to home, he didn't think twice about it.

"I love to work," Joe says. "And I don't feel any pressure to do anything but what the coach asks me to do and help my team out any way I can. I'm ready to go."

CHRIS BOSH

CHRIS BOSH

Chris Bosh is one of the funniest, most charismatic players in the NBA. He could have been a talk show host, a politician, or even a comedian! Remember his Internet video before the All-Star Game two years ago? He pretended to be a character named Chris W. Bosh, a used-car salesman who begged fans to vote him onto the team.

> **"They basically told me I have the right to push everybody else when some guys are slacking off some days."**

Luckily for his fans, Chris chose basketball for his career! For now, at least, Christopher Wesson Bosh is happy to be the best player and team captain for the Toronto Raptors, who chose him with the fourth pick in the 2003 NBA Draft. The 6-10 forward likes to win the game more than anything else.

"The mood always lightens after a win," Chris says. "People are nicer, the food tastes better, practice is a lot more fun."

Few athletes have the ability to play at a high level and be the leader of their teams, but Chris is one of them. At Lincoln High School in Dallas, Texas where Chris was born on March 24, 1984, he was the team captain in his junior and senior years. In his final year, the team had a 40-0 record and captured the state title. He also was a member of the National Honor Society and graduated with honors.

Chris starred at Georgia Tech University before he turned pro. It took only four seasons for him to have more points, free throws, rebounds, and blocked shots than any player in Raptors history. In the dictionary, the word "consistent" should have his picture next to it. In the last four seasons, he averaged 22.7, 22.3, 22.6, and 22.5 points per game.

It usually takes awhile for a young player to become a leader, but at 25 years of age, Chris welcomes the challenge.

"They basically told me I have the right to push everybody else when some guys are slacking off some days," Chris says. "They want me to do a better job of getting on them and demanding the best of them, because that's what all the great players do — they demand the best out of their teammates and make everybody better."

DIRK NOWITZKI

DIRK NOWITZKI

Almost every NBA team has at least one player who was born in Europe or another foreign country on its roster, but it wasn't always that way. Somebody had to pave the way for them. Somebody had to prove that an outsider was good enough to play in the best basketball league in the world.

One of those people was Dallas Mavericks sharpshooter Dirk Nowitzki, whom many consider to be the most talented European player in NBA history.

Born in Würzburg, Germany, Dirk Werner Nowitzki (pronounce it Noh-VIT-skee) wanted to play pro ball since he was a kid. "When I was just 17, I joked with my dad, 'I wanna become a basketball pro,'" the 7-foot forward recalls. "Of course, I didn't know at that time it would be the NBA, but that was all I could think of."

In 1998, Dirk began to live his dream, as the Milwaukee Bucks drafted him in the first round then traded him to the Mavericks a short time later. At the time, he was barely 20 years old and had a lot to learn about his new league.

Some people called him Irk Nowitzki, because there was no D (as in defense) in his game, they said. The taunts didn't bother Dirk, though. They only made him want to work even harder to become a more complete player.

Years later, Dirk is sort of like the sunset — every night you know what to expect of him. He'll play 30-something minutes. He'll score 20-something points. He'll grab close to 10 rebounds. Most important, his team will usually win the game.

> **"When I was just 17, I joked with my dad, 'I wanna become a basketball pro.'"**

An eight-time All-Star and one-time Most Valuable Player, Dirk has accomplished almost everything except an NBA championship in his career. He came close in the 2005-06 season when the Mavericks advanced to the NBA Finals but lost to the Miami Heat in six games.

Dirk was disappointed to fall short of his goal, but in the big picture, he has done something even more impressive. He has made it easier for foreign talents to play professional basketball in this country, and the game is better because of it.